I0040974

Starting Simple: Sales Compensation

Christopher Goff

Christopher Goff

The information provided in this book is for informational purposes only. The information and/or documents contained in this book should never be used without first consulting with a professional to determine what may be best for your individual needs.

The publisher and the author do not make any guarantee or other promise as to any results that may be obtained from using the content of this book. To the maximum extent permitted by law, the publisher and the author disclaim any and all liability in the event any information, commentary, analysis, opinions, advice and/or recommendations contained in this book prove to be inaccurate, incomplete or unreliable, or result in any losses.

Content contained or made available through this book is not intended to and does not constitute legal advice or investment advice and no attorney-client relationship is formed. The publisher and the author are providing this book and its contents on an "as is" basis. Your use of the information in this book is at your own risk.

STARTING SIMPLE: SALES COMPENSATION

All rights reserved.

Copyright 2022 © CHRISTOPHER GOFF

ALL RIGHTS RESERVED. This book contains material protected under International and Federal Copyright Laws and Treaties. Any unauthorized reprint or use of this material is prohibited. No part of this book may be reproduced or transmitted in any form or by any means, electronic or mechanical, including photocopying, recording, or by any information storage and retrieval system without express written permission from the author / publisher.

Paperback ISBN
979-8-9862249-0-9

Gracey Mae
PUBLISHING

For

My Love

Tonya Lee

Christopher Goff

Contents

Christopher Goff

Introduction

Every success story is a tale of constant adaption, revision and change. A company that stands still will soon be forgotten.

-Sir Richard Branson

This book is for individuals and organizations who currently have no sales force. For start-ups and non-profits. For those smaller organizations that are looking to grow but have yet to make the leap. It is my intent that this book will help guide you through the early process of expansion through sales and illustrate how to determine financial objectives, responsibilities of the role, competitive pay practices, and experience sustainability over time. While the principles in this book can be used by an organization of any size--with or without an established sales team--the premise of this book is that your organization is starting from scratch with no sales employees yet hired. So the focus is on starting simple.

During my fifteen years in sales operations and compensation, I gained diverse experience in developing sales quotas, producing territory assignments, writing sales plan documents, and integrating sales teams from merger and acquisition activity. Much of that history was on-the-job training and a lot of hit and miss. I learned many sales and compensation practices from trial and error. These missteps gave me a great appreciation for human psychology, motivation, productivity, and decision-making. Throughout this book, I will present the learnings from my journey so that you don't have to go through the same trial and error.

What I discovered were some common problems and basic tenets that kept showing up in every situation. One of those tenets is that sales compensation is iterative. Not only is there no one-size-fits-all strategy, but the appropriate sales incentive structure for your organization is a function of:

- The role and responsibilities of the salesperson in procuring business
- The financial measures of a transaction
- Levels of performance
- Pay

And all of that is wrapped up in your unique culture only for a moment in time.

To make matters even more complex, that moment-in-time sales incentive is only effective for the strategy it was designed to serve. Once the organization pivots, it is very important to go back and vet your assumptions to ensure appropriate alignment and gain the desired outcomes.

When writing this book, I had to really think about what was important in getting started from scratch. However, this is not a one-and-done manual for setting up your sales strategy. Since sales strategy is iterative and requires continual evaluation, this book will ideally prompt questions and prepare you for the evolution of your sales organization. I hope that this book aids you in this journey.

—Christopher

Chapter 1:
Culture Matters

Determine what behaviors and beliefs you value as a company, and have everyone live true to them. These behaviors and beliefs should be so essential to your core, that you don't even think of it as culture
-    Brittany Forsyth

Corporate culture is the only sustainable competitive advantage that is completely within the control of the entrepreneur.
-    David Cummings

THERE ONCE WAS A SMALL COMPANY THAT sold various digital goods. They had been a small company for several years at this point, and all the original staff was still working there. One day, the owner and manager gathered everyone together to discuss company values. Everyone openly shared what they valued and voted on the four main values they wanted to shape their company culture around.

One of the values was growth. Everyone except Sherry, an operations manager, was on board with the value of growth. Deep down, Sherry felt threatened by the idea. She liked the company the way it was--small and comfortable. As the company grew, Sherry became more and more overwhelmed and frustrated. She became resentful of the different types of work she now had to do as the company scaled. Eventually, Sherry couldn't maintain the conflict with the organization's values and was let go for behavioral reasons. Her departure was not because she didn't do her job or show up on time, but because she was not aligned with company values and culture and continued to resist change. The culture evolved and Sherry felt left behind, desiring what once was. After some time, she could no longer hide that conflict and termination was inevitable.

Arguably the most important soft measure of an employee's success in a job is their alignment to the culture of the organization. Cultural alignment means sharing similar values and work principles with others in the company.

Is the culture clear in your organization today?

Does everyone in your circle understand and know why the product exists and how it serves the world? If not, now is the time to put in the effort to build out the "who we are" of your organization. It is especially important when it's time to expand. **New customers, through the voice of your new salesperson, will want to connect with the ethos of your product and people**. Sales guru and author, Anthony Iannarino, advocates that the main person needing the approval for hiring a salesperson is the client themselves. When you interview for a salesperson, it's important to keep in mind that they will be representing your company to the client. As Simon Sinek said, "People don't buy what you do; they buy why you do it. And what you do simply proves what you believe."

It is one thing to ensure that people know what to do and how to do it—that the team is pointed in the right direction and hearing the same action plan. **However, there is another important, less quantifiable gauge for the success of the salesforce: the collective feelings, attitudes, and values of the organization.**

The company ethos is an important factor in the success of your salesperson and the organization. Culture strengthens the alignment of people to a strategy. Positive culture is the glue that bonds a collective group of people within an organization to pursue actions in a unified and consistent fashion towards a common objective. Negative culture has the reverse effect. As we saw with Sherry, her internal conflict eventually created tension that could not be overcome.

A positive and congruent culture inside an organization matters. Introducing and harmon-izing the right people in the right positions in support of organizational strategy is the key to a successful salesforce. If all the players in the organization aren't aligned to the company values prior to the expansion of the company, it is unlikely that the new salesperson will be successful. A team that doesn't know how to perform against a "true north" of company values, attitudes, and priorities will not scale effectively. That is why culture is an important factor in hiring for the sales role within an organization.

With the loudening of the advertising/sales voice in your marketplace, the values and mission of the company will be tested, and your customers will ultimately respond. Customers will react either positively or negatively to their perception of your company's authenticity embodied in your salesperson. In most cases within the marketplace, they are both the first impression and last impression. Make sure the salesperson presents themselves in sync with the company's values and gives your customer the experience you want them to have. Ultimately, the prospects and customers will let you know if they believe the authenticity of the purpose of the company, product, and people. If your company's values don't line up with the actions of your salesperson, your customers will vote with their feet and leave. You may be able to fool them once, but you won't fool them for long. The inconsistency of values can only be hidden for a short time. Be sure to bring on a salesperson that is aligned with your culture, otherwise the customer experience will suffer along with your financial performance.

With a company culture established, you are in a much better position to recruit talent. And talent will find it much easier to find you. People want to work at an organization where they are aligned with their values. As Abraham Maslow taught us, once we satisfy the basic physiological and safety needs that come with pay and a safe work environment, there are psychological and self-fulfillment needs that must be met. Those include belongingness, accomplishment, prestige, and ultimately achieving one's full potential. In the right work setting and cultural atmosphere, an individual will be able to unleash their creative potential while strengthening the organization through purposeful work. This is why culture is so important. **If you find people who are aligned with your company values, you will not need to remind them how they should work at work.** The right person will want to be part of building something bigger than themselves through the tough work and difficult times because of the strength of the culture and the mission and values that are omnipresent.

Be culture forward. Wear it everywhere, especially in the recruitment process for talent, so that someone can opt out quickly if they don't align.

One last note on culture. The tone that is set by

the leaders and founder of an organization will be felt throughout. Ensure that the individuals that can influence the temperature in the room are aligned with the culture you want to have going forward. Be sure that they are in sync with these values. If they aren't, it is time for them to move on.

Like in the scenario with Sherry, the people, processes, and values that got you to this point won't necessarily move you forward. It is important to acknowledge that people bring diverse strengths to differing aspects of the life cycle of an organization. **Cultures and companies evolve, and sometimes people do not.** It really is better for both of you to cut ties before the relationship sours. It may seem harsh in the moment, but you will both be happier. They will be free to pursue other organizations where their values better align.

By the way, I'm not saying to go fire everyone who doesn't agree with you. If that's what you read, then likely you will need to pull out the mirror to improve the culture problem. **Instead, provide direction and vision for the value system that will support the organization you want to become.** Then, ensure that your leadership is aligned. You will need those leaders to help ensure the rest of the organization follows along for the journey.

Ultimately your culture should include openness and transparency, generous recognition for the work being done, an atmosphere of acceptance and mutual respect, and inspirational leadership along with any other values that are unique to your organizational dynamics. Don't just copy another company. Be authentic and aspirational. Embody the type of person (and organization) you will become in the journey of your growth.

With alignment better understood, let's move on to a financial analysis of what your company can afford in terms of hiring a salesperson.

Homework
1. List 3-5 values that could help set your company and your new salesperson up for success.

Chapter 2:
Know Your Numbers

Mathematics is not about numbers, equations, computations, or algorithms: it is about understanding.
- William Paul Thurston

Mathematics may not teach us to add love or subtract hate, but it gives us hope that every problem has a solution.
- Anonymous

ASSUMING YOU'VE REACHED THE POINT WHERE you're officially in need of a salesperson, and your company is on solid footing in terms of values and culture, the next step is determining whether you can afford a salesperson. Believe it or not, a lot of young companies fail to take this first step, and they pay for it in the long run.

First thing's first–take the time to do the math!

<u>What can you afford?</u>

The first step is validating what your organization can afford to pay someone in guaranteed compensation (base/basic salary) for a specified length of time given your existing run-rate revenue and cost structure.

There are several ways to calculate what your company can afford in base pay. However, most companies will look at the monthly gross receipts or recurring revenue level. Whatever cash in-flow structure best represents your organization, you must understand the cost impact associated with bringing on an additional resource. On a monthly basis, what amount of money can the organization afford right now, and for how long? What would need to change in order to afford more?

Depending on where you are in your organizational growth and background, this may seem like an unnecessary step to cover, but in my experience it is precisely the place to start.

Larger organizations may have the regular cash flow to insulate themselves from the downturns and inefficiencies of business performance. Smaller organizations do not have that luxury, and time spent preparing is worth every moment to ensure accuracy of execution.

What are you expecting?

Next, what level of variable pay (sales incentive) can the organization afford to provide? And how? What are the conditions required in order to have the incremental cash flow to pay the newly hired salesperson?

Obviously the reason for bringing on a sales resource is to produce incremental revenue or accelerate the speed with which revenue is generated for the organization...in other words, to make more money faster.

However, keep in mind that the salesperson will need to cover the cost of their own position. At what point is the salesperson fully covering their costs and becoming profitable? Think of this like a break-even point at each hire. You need to understand when it is financially viable (and at what level of sales performance) to bring on a salesperson at each point of expansion.

Variable pay or pay-at-risk needs to be thought through both in terms of the organization's objective and the value of each transaction:

- Are some transactions being sold by the salesperson less valuable than others (whether in size, scope, profitability, etc.)?

- What is each marginal sale worth to the organization?
- What is the salesperson's role in procuring it?
- What can you afford to pay the salesperson at varying levels of performance?

These questions may seem overwhelming, but by taking the time to address them one by one, you'll be laying the groundwork for a sustainable compensation plan that can evolve as your company grows.

Total Compensation

The sum of guaranteed pay plus variable pay is called Total Target Cash compensation (TTC); you may have also heard this referenced in sales as "OTE" or On-Target Earnings, but for the purpose of this book, we'll be using TTC.

Compensation has other components that can also be added into this equation depending on regulatory, cultural, and geographic guidelines. But to keep it simple, we will just use the simple equation of:

Guaranteed Pay + Variable Pay = TTC.

Adding the base salary and sales incentive target should provide a perspective on your organization's ability to pay associated with a certain level of performance. Generally, the next step would be to look at the labor market competitive pay levels for the sales job, but first we need to spend some time defining the job content and fit.

What's your market?

Now that you have some perspective on your ability to afford a sales resource, let's take a look at the market that your organization covers. How will your salesperson pursue business in your target marketplace? How does your organization attract revenue, and will the salesperson cover the market differently than previous individuals have? I will cover more of this in later chapters, but for now, the questions are meant to get you thinking about your market demographics, the size of the deals, and the probability of your salesperson's success in persuading those in the marketplace to transact.

Your market segment is determined or defined as all of the customers that fit the profile of your target customer demographics that would benefit from your product or service offering. It is further clarified by proximity and scope. As an example, all marketing consultants that service firms under 100M in revenue or marketing consultants in the Northeastern, United States.

Defining Transaction Values

Deal size or value means quantifying the average transaction. Ask yourself:

- Does the size of the deal vary based on certain aspects of the customer demographic?
- Is it a fixed amount, or does it vary substantially based on the size of the client company, complexity of the offer, location,

etc.?
- Will those factors differ once the new salesperson is on board?
- Will the salesperson be able to modify the deal value or expand the size of these transactions in some way?

Another important step is looking at the propensity for customers to buy from you.

- What percentage of your defined market segment will purchase from you today? Or this fiscal year?
- Will you be able to win more business with the new salesperson?

Defining how and why is an important thing here. Your new salesperson will be able to test those assumptions very quickly.

Example

What if you assume you are able to convert 5% of the market this year? Compare that to what you were able to win last year. Does the difference seem like a reasonable progression?

Note: this isn't about win rate but true penetration or conversion of the total market.

Think about your competitors. Have you accounted for their influence? What does your influence on the buyer's decision look like currently? If so, does a new salesperson influence this outcome differently?

Let's suppose your clients are marketing consultants in the United States that service firms under 100 million in revenue. Say there are 365 of them. There are also an additional 95 in the Northeastern United States that service firms over 100 million in revenue beyond that. That is 460 potential customers.

These customers range in size from individual consultants to very large organizations housing many creative staff, administration, and client support, and consultants. Your product is software that helps staff project manage the development of creative product solutions that include video, graphic, print, written, and a variety of other creative mediums. The offering varies in size based on the number of staff and projects being worked. You have found that it averages about $1,500 per artist/creative staff per year, and the deal size generally varies between $4,500 and $15,000 per customer in annual revenue.

You believe you can penetrate the market at a rate of 8.5% in this first year with the help of your new salesperson. On your own, you would probably only be able to address 3% of that market.

Firms <100M	365
Northeast Firms	95
Total Market	460

Deal Size Range (Per Year)

6,000		18,000	
Market Penetration Rate		Market Penetration Rate	
3%	8.50%	3%	8.50%
Market Penetration Amount Ranges		Market Penetration Amount Ranges	
82,800	234,600	248,400	703,800

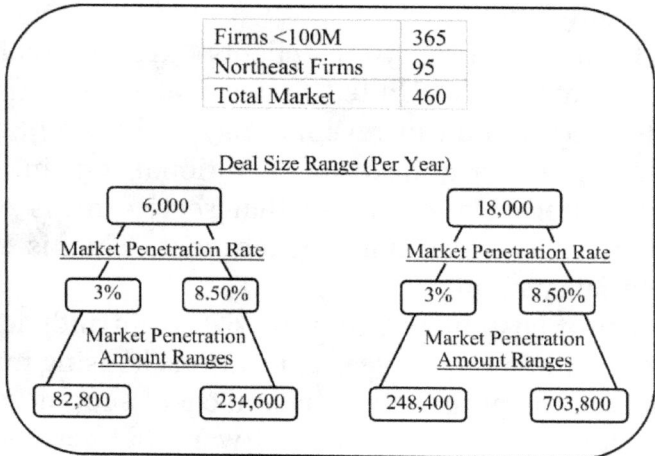

The importance of this exercise is to quantify the variability in the range of financial outcomes you can achieve. There is an 8.5x difference between the lowest level of penetration and the highest level of penetration assumed. The value of the salesperson's contribution will likely be somewhere in between. There are always chances of underperformance and overperformance, but given the questions that you just answered, you should be within a solid range of expected performance. Ultimately understanding this range will be a valuable data point as we continue to cover pay levels.

Beyond the market value and competitive dynamics, you will also want to consider the time required to recruit and train a salesperson. What is that time delay? Be sure to align the reasonable expectations after the lag time of getting up to speed. Remember that it always takes longer than you expect. Our estimates on time required always fall short of the actual time needed to accomplish anything of complexity.

To recap, it is important to acknowledge both the expected revenue stream and the profitability of the expansion of a channel of business. Is it going to be similar to or different from the past? Be sure to keep in mind that expected revenues will come with new costs, given the expansion of the sales force and the additional supporting resources and processes that may also be required in the pursuit of this new sales channel.

Best Practice: Have all of this ironed out <u>before</u> hiring that first salesperson. Without the financial plan in place, the rest of the steps in this book will be less effective. More importantly, you will reduce the probability of success for the salesperson and thereby the organization. **What comes from this financial modeling is clarity, alignment, and expectations.** While you can get there without it, more preparation will get you there in the shortest distance.

With alignment better understood, let's move on to clarity of work.

<u>Homework:</u>
1. Before continuing through the rest of the book, do some quick market-validation of your financial model using the questions in this chapter.
2. Identify the range of the potential value your salesperson may bring. This datapoint will be helpful when reading the rest of the book.

Chapter 3:
What is Job Content?

Clarity precedes success
- Robin Sharma

JOB CONTENT IS THE OUTLINE OF the role and responsibilities of the position. It can be simple or complex based on the job functions. The content of the job describes what, how, where, and when. It may even describe the who and the why. A good job description provides clarity for the applicant and your future growth. I use the term future growth because you are documenting the expected knowledge, skills, and abilities of a sales job that you need to assist you in the next phase of organization evolution. The position plays a part in that growth, and you want those forward-looking intentions to be as clear as possible.

When crafting a job description, it can be tempting to "borrow" from LinkedIn, Indeed, Monster, or the hundreds of other sites that post sales jobs. I don't recommend doing this because no other organization is identical to yours. While it absolutely gets a job description done quickly, it misses the mark on being able to tell the story of exactly what you need from the individual who will be successful in this job and in supporting your organization. You miss the opportunity to tell the story of your successful future and how they fit into it.

Instead of borrowing, take the time--although it may seem tedious--to describe what it is that your organization needs to be successful, and how this position will support that strategy. It is important to clearly articulate what role this job will play in that process.

The job content should help answer many of these questions:

- What does the person need to do on a daily basis?
- How does this individual pursue sales, and in what segment or with what type of customer?
- Where should they focus their time and attention in building a pipeline of deals?
- Who should they be interfacing with both internally and externally?

- When do they engage with customers and/or prospects?

It is important to be clear on the purpose and mission of the organization. Answering the question of why the organization does what it does will ensure alignment from the right individual to support that pursuit. These questions are far more than simply talking points. The purpose of answering them is to clarify the objectives of the organization and the salesperson's role in supporting those objectives.

The exercise of answering all of these questions will assist you in many ways. First, it forces your organization to explain the sales actions and market coverage. Second, it helps you write a strong job description that will attract the right candidates. Lastly, it creates a clearly defined yardstick for success along the path to growth. By writing out the job description from scratch and answering these questions, you'll build clarity both for yourself and your candidates, and you'll ultimately create alignment.

A completed job description will also help you determine what a job is worth in the labor market. That job description and the underlying compensatory factors will assist you in determining the most common job titles that correspond with the details of your job content. You may already be fully aware of the title that you want to advertise for, but there has certainly been an evolution of titles and the underlying assumptions (and biases) about the respons-ibilities of those jobs.

As an example, a Business Development Representative (BDR) in many industries is a telephone-based or fully virtual lead generation role that focuses on maximizing the volume of prospect engagement. In other industries that same Business Development terminology refers to a field sales (travel-based) role that owns the entire sales cycle from end-to-end. And still other industries consider the terminology synonymous with marketing and collateral support or even corporate partnership and reseller management.

In that same vein, the "size" of the title changes depending on the level of interaction and influence with the sales prospect. In the financial sector, it isn't uncommon to have Vice Presidents or Executive Vice Presidents for the entry-level sales role both because it is common practice but also because of the perception that it's easier to access prospects at similar hierarchical (internal title) levels. If you are selling to Directors, your salesperson's title may simply need to be "Sales Director." Titles don't tell you the job content, but they do help you recruit.

The bottom line is, **make sure your job description aligns with the common vernacular for titles and levels in your industry and your niche offering**. It is okay to stand out, but you also need to ensure you don't lose out on access to talent that is searching for very specific titles and levels of progression.

You will benefit from spending some time on

those same career sites I advised you not to copy from. Look at what your competitors are posting for jobs and titles. Reach out to recruiters and friends and associates in sales and gain their opinions. You will find it to be an extremely worthwhile exercise in understanding the dynamics of the language that is used in your job description and ensure that it is clear, aligns with your strategy, and is engaging enough to attract attention from prospective employees.

While you're crafting your job description, it is also important to construct the broader expectations of the role. This includes how the role interacts with internal and external stakeholders. From an internal perspective this may include, but is not limited to, activities such as lead development, writing proposals, advising on contract language, leading demonstrations, and maintaining data in customer relationship management (CRM) tools. CRM activities can include quoting pricing and technical specifications, running reports, or building a sales forecast. Additionally, the internal stakeholders may include the product, marketing, operations, or legal team members to name a few. An expectation of how the salesperson is intended to interact with each of them to get deals into the organization paves the way for success in the role.

External stakeholders may include partners or resellers, industry experts, or simply procurement managers or the prospect/client. Your salesperson will need clear direction on how to interact with them according to the etiquette of your industry. Creating clear expectations about how and when to engage with prospects, customers, and any additional external resources will help your salesperson be successful as quickly as possible.

Another important aspect of the job description is defining the salesperson's level of autonomy. This includes items like discount authority and the ability to modify terms and conditions. You may not yet have documented these items, but there is no time like the present. Setting an expectation of what authority you are willing to delegate or defining what a "good" deal looks like is better determined earlier rather than later.

As an example, if you expect the new salesperson to take over all day-to-day sales activity upon hire, the following questions should be covered:

- What is the existing sales process and daily disciplines that you would train that individual on?
- Who do you currently call on and why?
- What number of follow-up interactions does it normally take to complete a sale?
- What sort of marketing collateral has been used to persuade a customer to purchase?
- What type of communication and medium has proven successful to date?

If there are no lessons learned from the current sales process, then be transparent in the advertisement and with the candidate that a process needs to be created. You want to ensure you hire a person who can help you develop that model to allow for scalability over time rather than someone that expects the model to be completed upfront. On the flip side, if there is a great deal of proven success and documented transferable skills, collateral, and daily actions, then you will want to look for the individual who can focus on execution of that tried-and-true workflow and can accelerate the timeframe for getting up to speed.

A byproduct of finalizing the job content is a job description that will touch on many of the items below:

- Job duties and responsibilities which clarify the type of work and engagement with customers.
- Qualifications/Requirements that are both minimum and desired. Those include education, knowledge, skills, capabilities, and competencies.
- Performance measures of the role that include items like achieving sales target, new logo acquisition, development of pipeline, accuracy in forecasting, etc.

While we are on the topic of job description, it is important to acknowledge the trend of transparency of pay. It is better to be open and clear about expectations rather than have people feel like they're going into a bait and switch scenario in the recruiting process. Like conflict, it is better to get it out of the way a.s.a.p. and not put internal culture at risk because of it.

While it may seem uncomfortable at first, many organizations are moving in the direction of pay transparency. That includes clear messaging about levels of pay for both base and variable. Do your direct competitors advertise pay levels? If so, you may have little choice to ensure competitiveness. If not, you have a little more control. Be sure to use that information you gained from researching your competitor practices to help gauge your positioning in the marketplace. Start by looking at your competitors and where you would expect to source your talent. Which industry, which companies, and what background, education, and experience? Either direction you take, ensure the decision on pay transparency aligns with your cultural values around pay equity and competitiveness.

An example of a simple job content statement:

Remote salesperson (Account Executive) in pursuit of incremental/new business. Travel-based role. Accountable for selling marketing software direct business to business (B2B).

Role definition/expansion of the job description:

The coverage model is out-bound, field-based (travel required), and accountable for acquiring new business logos. The salesperson will manage the deal from end-to-end (full sales cycle accountability) and need to uncover their own leads, negotiate through all phases of the deal, and manage the close process. Knowledge of finance and marketing operations. Bachelor's degree in Business preferred. Experience in a sales role for a minimum of 3 years required. The role is responsible for persuading and influencing buyer decisions. Corporate marketing functions experience preferred. Familiarity with the B2B sales process is required.

Now that we have covered the clarity of the job, let's talk about pay.

 Homework:

1. If you haven't already done so, take the time to define the job and its responsibilities. Be sure to cover the who, what, where, when, why, and how of the job.

2. Identify the lessons learned thus far in your revenue acquisition journey that can be transferable to your new sales hire.

3. Take the time to self-evaluate your current position in the market versus your competitors. How do you rank/compare? What needs to be overcome?

Chapter 4:
Pay & Mix

If you hire good people, give them good jobs, and pay them good wages generally something good is going to happen

- James Sinegal

NOW THAT YOU KNOW WHAT YOU can afford and have a completed job description in hand, you will be able to see how your job compares to other listings. Hopefully the other job listings will validate your assumptions of projected total pay package for the job. I'll address what to do when they don't a little later.

I'll assume at this point, you probably don't have

a formal internal job structure, so the first step is to get grounded in what external jobs look like, and what their going rate of pay is. I'd start with a few free sources like the following:

www.bls.gov Under the Occupational Employment and Wage Statistics section you can see what the actual pay has been like for various occupations. It is a good starting point.

https://www.onetonline.org/ A good resource to help develop the job content and to see how that job content is aligned to a particular job title. The great thing about this database is that you can get started with a simple search on "sales" to view all of the different occupations that align to that keyword.

www.repvue.com is a repository for SaaS sales jobs. They collect their data in partnership with companies to manage recruitment but also collect data from individuals to supplement a ranking of organizations in that sector. If you are sourcing talent from the software/technology sector, these are the pay levels that you will need to be aware of. This will aid in both the pay amounts and the job description elements.

https://www.payscale.com/products/payfactors-free/ is a 100% HR-sourced, employer-validated compensation database. You can get started by market pricing a couple of jobs for

free and can use your specific industry or
location.

A couple of additional options include:
Salary.com, Glassdoor.com, Indeed.com,
Salarylist.com, Salary-expert.com. These websites
will provide some further insight. Word of caution,
however, is that many of these are also crowd-sourced
datasets that may illustrate expectations of pay as well
as actual pay. That can make accuracy a bit more
difficult to achieve since what is free is not always
validated by employers or W2 wage data.

When reviewing the multiple data sources, you
want to pay attention to the job content, job title,
industry, location, experience, education, and any
unique competencies that differentiate that job from
the one you are comparing it to. Ultimately, it is better
to collect multiple data points to address the volatility
of the data collected.

When analyzing other job listings and collecting
data, pay specific attention to compensable factors,
total compensation, and pay mix.

Compensable Factors

With a completed job description, you will be able
to reference comparable jobs in the market and on job
listing sites. Compensable factors are distinct
characteristics of the job that elevate or reduce the
value of the job in the labor market. These same
compensable factors are what will be differentiators
in the level of job once multiple jobs exist. Think of

items like applicable sales or industry experience, communication and present-ation skills, level of autonomy and responsibility exercised, complexity of duties, education/ training, working conditions, supervision/ direction required. Each of these are areas that will illustrate different levels of jobs in the marketplace (and can then be used in the future as the organization grows to differentiate internal job levels). Essentially, each of these different components documented in the job description provides insight into the comparable level of job. Think of this concept of level progression in terms of titles like Assistant, Associate, Professional, Senior, and Chief. The underlying compensable factors determine the level of job in comparison to both internal structures and market data levels.

Human resource or compensation professionals use the combined compensable factors to determine the job worth in the labor market and how it stacks up against market data. The compensable factors are the nitty-gritty within the job description that helps connect the dots to the compensation amount. This process is generally referred to as job matching and market pricing. A similar exercise focused on internal levels and equity is called job evaluation.

Total Compensation and Pay Mix
The components of pay that are most important are the guaranteed component (base salary) and the variable pay component. Generally, variable pay is communicated in the form of a commission rate,

bonus percentage, or target sales incentive amount. There are also some sales jobs that are base salary only and others that are 100% commission only. I will focus only on sales roles that have both a base salary and variable component.

Pay mix refers to the amount of base salary relative to the total target cash compensation. As an example, if a sales job has a base salary of $40,000 and variable pay at target (at the point of achieving 100% of the sales objective) of $10,000 the job has a mix of 80/20 or 80% base salary and 20% variable pay. What this means is that the job has a total target cash compensation amount of $50,000,

Many websites share base salary and the variable pay amounts. What you are ultimately after in the data collection process is the total target cash compensation for the position to compare to what you can afford. If you can collect insights on the variable pay and mix, you can understand what others are doing so you can decide how competitive you want to be. One thing to note, however, is that the mix is entirely up to you. Companies rarely have exactly the same mix but, more importantly, the mix you select should be a function of some of the factors you will learn about as you continue to read through this book. You should consider what others are doing in the labor market. However, you should also make sure your TTC compensation aligns with your compensation philosophy.

When collecting pay data, you will collect information on the base salary, target incentive, total target cash compensation. You will also want to collect any information you can capture on actual pay as well. That usually comes in the form of actual variable incentive and total actual cash compensation. Actual pay just means what was actually paid to the employee. It provides insight into the performance against quota and the percentage of the target pay that is being delivered to the employee. When looking at traditional compensation surveys, we collect various percentile ranges like 10th, 25th, 50th, 75th, and 90th to help us understand this distribution of performance in greater detail. It is unlikely that you will find too much of this free but **when really digging into competitive pay you are searching for the details of what people actually make versus how the jobs are advertised**. Actual pay data is a gauge of what cash is being delivered to prospective employees for similar jobs but also provides insight into the prevalence of other plan components (predominately the pay curve) that we will discuss further in the coming chapters.

The outcome from this data collection exercise should be a range of numbers. This isn't a fixed point because no two companies pay exactly the same way. You will want to land somewhere in that range to stay competitive. And over time you will want to develop a pay philosophy that will more explicitly align your organization to a certain point in that pay data. Most organizations target the 50th percentile as the common practice.

Internal Equity

You need to account for both market competitiveness and internal equity. Market competitiveness looks at the mixture of survey data, job postings, and sales compensation guidelines for the type of job. Essentially, it is validating that the compensation package you are offering is at a competitive level to attract, retain, and motivate individuals to be successful in the job. Internal equity is the alignment to any pre-existing compensation guidelines and philosophies that your organization has. Is the pay package equitable with other jobs of a certain level?

Ultimately this becomes more important as the organization grows in population. With more sales roles, there is a responsibility to ensure no pay disparities exist among employees within each sales role. In sales this includes a consideration on the base salary, target incentive, total target cash compensation, and equitable opportunity to earn under the sales plan. That may include a review of territorial assignments or other underlying aspects that impact actual pay delivered as well. Keep this in mind as the team grows and evolves.

How Do You Stack Up?

With a little understanding of what the market looks like, let's revisit the thoughts from chapter two. How does your financial model compare to the base salaries that you are seeing in the market data? How does the variable compare? Are there gaps? And if so, are they significant?

If you can't afford the base, would you be able to make it up with a more aggressive variable pay model? If so, consider a more aggressive payout for overperformance in the sales plan or accelerated cash payments with sustained sales success. I'll get to these nuances of design in greater detail in chapters six and seven.

If you can't afford the variable then you may need to revisit your financial model and see if there are any changes that can be made to allow for more room. I'd also consider the short-term versus long-term aspects of this investment and if there can be more front-end loaded expenses or if there are other creative opportunities for long-term profit-sharing for the sales employee.

Practical Options on Pay & Mix

Your individual mix is as much about culture and competitive levels as it is the fit in your financial models. If your level of affordability doesn't match the level of compensation in the market then there are a few alternatives to consider

1. Modification to the coverage model
2. Downgrading the position
3. Ensuring greater reward for performance (upside)

Coverage Model

The coverage model is how you define your salesperson's pursuit of business and engagement with clients in your particular market space. There are many other books on the topic, so I am not going to spend a lot of time on it. But if affordability is the issue, adjusting the coverage model is a good alternative. Think creatively and determine whether the initial financial model is in sync with the learnings from the market data. After learning the market cost associated with the role, reconsider how the salesperson could approach the customer differently and modify the assumptions. This would require an adjustment to the financial model and the job functions. As an example, if your initial thoughts were that you needed an enterprise field salesperson to pursue business, but your financial model requires substantially lower total pay based on your initial data collections, look at modifying the way that your salesperson procures business. This may mean modifying the coverage to outbound telephone-based or lead generation only sales coverage instead. Do your competitors have inside sales? Do you believe you can make an impact by pursuing an alternative route? If the last few years have taught us anything, there is more than one way to get work done!

<u>Downgrading The Position</u>

Another alternative is to consider the level of the position. This can be done either by itself or in combination with the coverage model. You can reduce the requirements and expectations of the role to a lower level. This would be as simple as requiring less experience or setting a lower financial expectation that is commensurate with a lower pay level.

This is captured through the modification of the compensable factors in the job description. From the previous example, your initial thought may have been to require 10 years of sales experience and some graduate level education. But upon your market research, you found that your financial model would not fund that level role. You then have to revisit your job description and get in sync with what your budget can truly handle. Perhaps it is 2-5 years of sales experience and no degree.

Greater Upside Potential

This is the deliberate effort to deliver more pay over the financial objective of the salesperson than would normally be the case (either from the financial model or the market). This could equate to more aggressive accelerators or milestone bonuses, or other pay mechanics which I will get into in greater detail in Chapter 6. What I am not advocating for is the very questionable action of hiding unattainable earnings above quota as a way of affording to employ someone. What I am advocating is a creative review of the design of your financial model to significantly reward high performance on a reasonable objective that wasn't in sync with your initial financial model. This can be as simple as "enriching the pot," marketing the job to job-seekers, and being transparent about the affordability concerns your organization has.

Where affordability is a challenge, especially as it relates to the base salary component of pay, one of the simplest decisions is to model a richer variable pay plan. That strategy may include steps or tiers to acknowledge the financial needs of the business. Again, transparency of your financial model and the alignment of the job to those criteria will aid in bringing in the right people at the right level with the right set of expectations.

Now that we have covered pay, let's consider sales objectives.

<u>Homework:</u>
1. Try your hand at collecting market data with your completed job description. Remember to focus on the total target compensation, the mix, and the actual pay information where possible.
2. Validate that the compensation level for the job is congruent with the financial model. Revisit the financial model if necessary and consider the options discussed at the end of the chapter.

Chapter 5: Objectives

High achievement always takes place in the framework of high expectation
- Charles Kettering

High expectations are the key to everything
- Sam Walton

TARGETS, QUOTAS, GOALS, PERFORMANCE measures, and objectives are the terms commonly used to identify the most important expected results and outcomes for an organization. Objectives may come in the form of acronyms like KPIs (Key Performance Indicators), KSIs (Key Success Indicators), KRAs

(Key Results Area), CSFs (Critical Success Factor), or OKRs (Objective and Key Results). In this book we will predominantly use the term "objectives" to define expectations placed on the salesperson.

Whatever your preferred acronym, these objectives are at the core of the sales incentive plan. They establish a guide for the salesperson that directs their behaviors and actions. And they also establish a point in the pay curve where the expected variable pay (target incentive) will be paid out in full. Objectives will guide how you develop an incentive plan that has particular mechanics for pay across differing levels of sales activity. The performance objective is the point that differentiates your approach and philosophy for pay for underperformance and pay for overperformance. I will cover this more thoroughly in the next chapter, as I go into greater details on plan mechanics.

Types of Targets

Sales objectives generally come in the form of financial objectives. Other types of objectives include sales process activities or forecast progression milestones. In your organization, you will need to focus on what objectives and goals are the most meaningful so you can be clear about what winning looks like to your salesperson. Sometimes choosing targets is straightforward, and other times it requires a bit more creativity.

For example, if the sales role is focused on support and lead generation for future revenue, your objectives will be related to activities such as calls, production of qualified leads, or meetings with prospects. As the role or business needs evolve, objectives may also include management of the pipeline in terms of volume, velocity, and ultimately closure. If that first sales role is focused on independent management of the sales process, then a measure of sales volume, expected or actual revenue, or profit margins may be more suitable.

	Financial Objectives	Sales Process Activities	Forecast Progression Milestones
Objective Type	Revenue	Calls	Sales cycle stage movement
	Profit	Sales Qualified Leads	Hand-off triggers between internal teams
	Gross Margin Percentage	Meetings	Customer/Prospect sign-off(s)
	Bookings/Sales Volume	Demonstrations	
		Proposals	
		Opportunities	
Focus	Volume Level Focused	Task Focused	Continuance Focused
	Quantity First, Quality secondary	Quality guidance required	Velocity of Deal Advancement

The important thing to remember is that the salesperson needs to be able to influence, if not fully control the objectives in order for them to be a meaningful metric for incentive pay. If the salesperson cannot move the needle, then you've given them the wrong objective.

Fairness

Before we get any further on sales quotas, let's be sure that we aren't saddling an unrealistic objective on the back of the new salesperson simply because it was in the financial model. The salesperson needs to be able to trust that the target is reasonable and achievable, and that starts with making it realistic for the timeframe and current status of the organization. The new salesperson will be more of a financial partner than almost any other employee in your organization. You do not want to jeopardize that relationship simply because unattainable expectations are established right out of the gate.

As an old sales leader of mine once said, "If the stick is too high, the dog just won't jump." Unrealistic targets will stagnate your growth potential and also give you a poor reputation for the next set of employees that come in the door.

Aggressive growth targets are natural, but the salesperson has to be able to believe that there is a path to achievement. Without that belief, it is unlikely the salesperson will be successful in meeting objectives or in being the best face to the customer that they can be.

Visibility

Not only does the salesperson need to believe in the possibility of success, they also need to clearly see the path to accomplishing it. That means providing them transparency around the financial model they are working under and also visibility of real-time performance levels against that model. When a salesperson is clear on their target, has the resources to achieve that target, and can clearly see the path forward, they feel motivated. And in sales, we want to ensure that the sales compensation reinforces this behavior as the salesperson progresses toward the target and beyond.

The value of a sales objective

Only around 50% of all sales employees achieve their objectives on an annual basis. In high performing sales organizations, around 60-70% are achieving quota. While this statistic is less meaningful with a population of only one, it should help illustrate the real challenges that the role faces across all organizations.

We all need goals or objectives in order to accomplish difficult things, and sales is no different. A salesperson's performance improves when there is a clear expectation of what needs to be delivered. Without that clear goal, the salesperson can't achieve their fullest potential in the job. However, there is a deeper value to setting reasonable targets and maintaining performance visibility–and that value is building trust through transparency. As

Stephen M. R. Covey states, "Trust is a powerful accelerator to performance and when trust goes up, speed also goes up while cost comes down." The development of trust enhances the efficacy of all employees, but you will see greater clear financial returns in the form of performance when trust is present in the organization.

Your organization will also need to follow through on the promises made throughout the employee lifecycle in order to develop and maintain organizational trust. The value of a sales objective is in adding clarity or purpose to the daily actions and behaviors that support the pursuit of a shared objective between the salesperson and the organization. Being transparent about how the sales objective was determined and sharing the underlying financial model will also aid in developing an environment where performance can be measured and managed. Trust is then reinforced by the organization delivering on its promises of pay for those aggressive sales targets being achieved. The optimal outcome is that the organization delivers on its promises, and the salesperson delivers on their objectives. High levels of performance by the salesperson and the follow through by the organization will develop a cycle of trust.

You may have heard of the old SMART acronym: Specific, Measurable, Achievable, Realistic, and Time-bound. All of those are important aspects for successful goal setting. It should go without saying that it is important to ensure that your new salesperson is motivated and encouraged to reach their objective. Make no mistake–if they miss their goals due to unrealistic expectations or lack of visibility, they will not stay. The target set must be believed and achieved in order for the organization to be successful in the short run and long run.

A few extra comments

Having more than one objective is fine, but keep in mind that more is not better. When selecting objectives, you have to acknowledge that split focus is a side effect of multiple goals. Less is always better. I'd advise you to only have one, if you can at all help it, and perhaps two if you absolutely must. Take the time to distill your priorities down to one primary objective of the job. Don't forget that this is a short-term incentive. Once the business changes, strategy shifts, and the role evolves, you will want to set objectives again. You are aligning what is important to the organization at this moment in time.

With the fine line of target setting understood, let's dive into the incentive plan mechanics.

Homework

1. Identify the #1 most important objective for your new salesperson. Is there a second or third objective that also makes the cut?
2. What is your timeline for achieving that objective?
3. What processes and support systems need to be in place to ensure the probability of success in achieving your targeted objective?

Chapter 6:
Plan Mechanics

The mechanics of putting one spot of color next to another, that is the fundamental thing.
- Charles Webster
Hawthorne

Our goals can only be reached through a vehicle of a plan, in which we must fervently believe, and upon which we must vigorously act. There is no other route to success.
- Pablo Picasso

SINCE WE HAVE COVERED THE IMPORTANCE of culture, the fundamental financial model, the job content, pay, and objectives, the next step is to dig into the nitty-gritty of the plan mechanics. This is where it all comes together.

Plan mechanics can take up a whole book in its own right. The aspects of a sales incentive plan design are numerous and complex. However, this book is intended as a practical guide to getting off on the best foot with your sales plan, so I am only going to focus on two types of sales incentive plans: a commission rate plan and a bonus plan.

The commission rate plan is exactly what it sounds like. It is a rate of pay against the financial objective established under your plan. In other words, it's a percentage of sales or revenue, or margin, that the salesperson earns when they meet your criteria for success. In most cases this is a simple fixed rate across all levels of performance, such as 10% of revenue or 5% of margin.

For example, your organization sells staffing hours. Your staffing hours model has a targeted gross profit of $10 per hour contracted. You may choose to pay your salesperson 10% on the margin which would translate into a sales incentive payment of $1 per hour of staffing services sold. The commission rate is fixed on a fixed margin built into your financial model. What is earned is a function of the number of hours sold by the salesperson and thereby the fixed margin amount procured. The rate you select can differ at certain levels of performance either over or under the target goal. This is analogous to the concept of a cost of sale. I refer to this as cost of sale because it is directly proportional to the volume sold by the salesperson.

On the other hand, a **bonus plan** establishes an amount of pay associated with delivering on an objective. There is a fixed amount of pay associated with the job. The quota or objective will vary, but the job has a certain level of pay regardless of the size of the goal. That target may differ across territory, time, or however the needs of the business evolve, but the target incentive remains fixed.

For example, based on your research of the market, the appropriate level of variable pay is $30,000 in annual target incentive or $2,500 per month for the role. The $2,500 per month would be the payout for 100% performance, regardless of what the quota is. This is analogous to the concept of cost of labor. I refer to it as a cost of labor because the cost of the plan is a function of the value of the job, rather than a function of how much of something is sold. The bonus plan is very effective when quotas and performance levels are unclear or unknown. It is also more common as companies grow in size and expect incremental productivity on an annual basis but want to manage cost.

With the two basic types of incentive plans covered, let's move on to the pay curve. **The pay curve is the relationship between pay and the performance levels in pursuit of the objective**. The most prominent points along that curve include zero, the threshold, the target, and the point of excellence.

The first point on the pay curve is zero (0%,0%). This is the point where there is zero payout and zero performance. It is the starting point of every pay curve.

The threshold is the point at which you first choose to pay sales incentive. Some sales plans delay payout of the first amounts of sales incentive until a certain level of performance is achieved. Let's say that you have a monthly sales bonus plan and no payout under the plan occurs until 50% of the sales quota is achieved.

The threshold can also be the point of zero. Essentially that means no threshold because earnings start from the beginning of performance. As you start out, I recommend that the threshold be the same as the zero point, unless you have sufficient history to determine and manage otherwise.

We have already covered the target, or 100% performance, of the objective. As a general rule this is where 100% of performance equates to 100% of payout of sales incentive under the plan. So the point is (100%,100%) on the pay curve.

The last point of the curve is the point of excellence. This is the point where your top performers would live and where you want more cash delivered to coincide with that high performance level. Over time, and with more data to support the decision, this is a point where you can design aggressive rewards to attract, retain, and motivate your top performers.

Best practice is that the threshold represents the point where 10% of your salesforce sits below. The point of excellence is where the top 10% of your sales team is performing. Regardless of your plan design you will always have at least two points to determine your pay curve (0%,0% and 100%,100%).

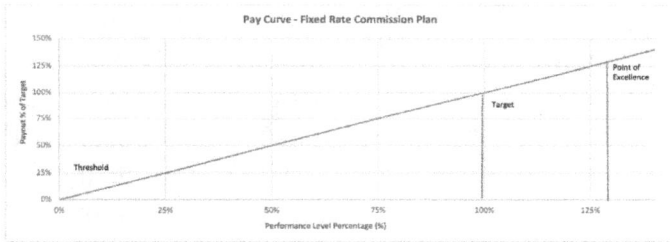

The figure above illustrates a straight line pay curve. The x-axis represents performance as a percentage of the target. The y-axis represents payout as a percentage of the target incentive. As you can see, the pay curve starts at (0%,0%). The threshold is also at (0%,0%). You wouldn't typically represent threshold on the pay curve at all when the threshold is at zero, but I am showing it for illustration here at zero. You will also see reference to the target. That target point of (100%,100%) represents the level of 100% performance and 100% payout. In the graphic, the point of excellence is 130% of the target for illustration. In this case, the point of excellence is at (130%,130%). The rate of pay is a straight line, representing a fixed rate across all levels of performance with pay starting from the very beginning of performance and continuing beyond the point of excellence.

With a population of only one, I would not focus much attention on the threshold or the point of excellence. The threshold is relevant when a certain level of performance is known and clearly expected. It is also an important aspect in your financial model. However, using a threshold is less appropriate in a completely unknown situation. Once you have an established business with more salespeople that are focused exclusively on run-rate business or client management, a threshold is a plan component that becomes far more valuable in the overall design.

The point of excellence is also a plan design element that becomes more valuable with a population greater than one, and after more performance data is collected. That is because with the point of excellence, you are intending to differentiate pay for your top performers at a rate that is higher than your lower and average performers. Once there is a broader population with more historical performance data, then the use of the threshold and point of excellence will be of greater value to you. Until that point, the plan philosophy should focus on simplicity of understanding and administration.

In the example above, the slope of the pay curve is 1--essentially a 1:1 ratio between performance and pay. More likely than not, that will serve your immediate needs. However, in order to be competitive, it is important to understand what market competitive plans offer.

The majority of sales plans across all industries have an accelerated rate over target. The most common accelerator rate is 2x or 3x. That means that the effective rate of pay is double or triple the base rate under target. That may not be accessible to your current financial model but it is important to be aware of this practice.

Ultimately, the selection of an accelerator is somewhat philosophical, role-specific, and should be supported by your financial model. Remember, if you **can't support it** financially, **don't proceed** with it. It is better to have a simple plan that you can have someone earn against than one you can't actually pay for.

In the previous paragraph, I mentioned that the rate for acceleration is role specific. Generally, when a role carries more risk, there is more reward. That reward comes in the form of pay mix (amount of variable at risk), objective (magnitude and type of financial measure), and leverage or upside opportunity. Sales roles that carry more risk generally have a path to greater upside potential. That means that a salesperson who is accountable for delivering and carrying a target for incremental revenue for the organization would have a higher accelerator than the salesperson responsible for lead generation. The magnitude of impact to the organization is captured in the decision. When establishing the eligibility for the types of pay curves specific to each sales role, you'll need to align with market competitive practices and with the expectations of the prospective salesperson.

Let's finish up the subject of pay above target by discussing leverage or upside. Leverage is the sales incentive that would be delivered between the 100% performance point and the point of excellence. It is represented as a multiple of the target incentive. Establishing a leverage gives us the slope of the pay curve in that range over target. As an example, if the variable pay for achieving 100% of the target is $15,000, and the leverage is 2x, then 2 x $15,000, or $30,000, would be expected to be paid to the salesperson achieving the point of excellence level of performance. If your point of excellence is 150%, then the accelerator rate is also 2x the rate from 0-100% of performance achieved. For our single rate plan, the leverage or "multiple" is the same as the slope of the pay curve at 1.

Let me break this down a bit further.

$15,000 is awarded for the first 100% of quota achieved. The next $15,000 is awarded for the next 50% of quota achieved because the point of excellence is 150%. Because 100%-150% is the same rate for half the level of percentage attainment, the slope of the accelerator (pay rate) is 2:1 that of the base rate. The leverage is used for both a bonus plan or for a commission rate plan. It is simply clarifying the pay curve and the relationship to performance above target.

To illustrate with a quota, let's assume the annual quota is $300,000 in revenue.

$15,000 / $300,000 is 5% (base rate under target)

$15,000 / $150,000 is 10% (rate up until the point of excellence)

The outcome is that we will cumulatively be paying $30,000 for $450,000 of revenue. This represents a blended rate of 6.67% through 150% of quota achieved.

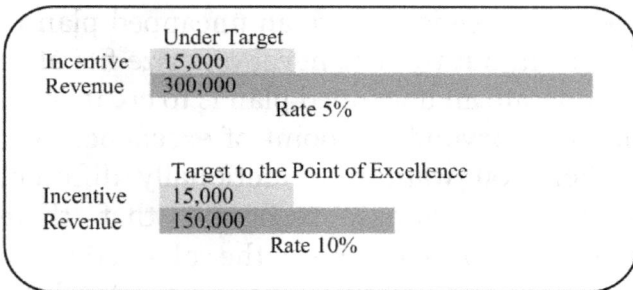

	Under Target
Incentive	15,000
Revenue	300,000
	Rate 5%

	Target to the Point of Excellence
Incentive	15,000
Revenue	150,000
	Rate 10%

To cap or uncap, that is the question

The pay beyond the point of excellence is also an important component. Ultimately, you want to design an incentive structure that encourages continued performance contingent on your business and the respective financial model.

Pay above the point of excellence will generally fall within a couple of categories: capped or uncapped. A capped plan stops paying after a certain level of performance. To be clear this is not best practice but is sometimes necessary.

An uncapped plan can have a couple of different options. Either the pay curve continues at a higher

67

rate of acceleration, continues at the same rate, or decelerates. All of these options have their place and purpose.

A capped plan can be appropriate when your business has known limitations or maximums; essentially where selling as much as possible isn't the *most* desired outcome/behavior. This may come in the form of manufacturing limitations or service capacity.

Best practice is to have an uncapped plan if you can afford it, but there is never one size fits all. One way to operate an uncapped plan is to create a higher acceleration beyond the point of excellence. You do this when you want to intentionally differentiate salesperson's earnings, recognize that there is incremental marginal value of the sales activity to the organization, and that there is some greater difficulty associated with this path of continued selling. If it is not more challenging for the salesperson to achieve, and the organization doesn't incrementally benefit (as in reduced incremental variable costs), then the further higher rate should not be selected. Essentially, if there is neither greater value to the organization nor greater difficulty in the performance by the individual, then there is little reason for a different rate above the point of excellence.

An uncapped plan can also offer a decelerated rate above the point of excellence. A decelerated rate is useful as it signals to the salesperson that there is value to the organization for over-performing, but that the incremental value to the organization declines at a certain point in time. This tells the seller that the declining marginal benefits of sales transactions to the business do not proportionally support the incremental sales effort over the point of excellence. This is a fairly common approach with organizations that have short (in terms of % of performance) but sizable accelerators to reward the highest performers. Best practice is to set the decelerator rate beyond the point of excellence at a rate higher than the base rate from zero or threshold to 100%. Rates below the base rate signal a complete halt to productivity which is rarely the message you want to send to the seller. As an example, if you have a simple 1:1 pay curve for 0-100% performance, but have a 3:1 pay curve from 100-150%, you will not want to have a 0.5:1 pay curve beyond 150%. Instead, you will want to have a rate between 1:1 and 3:1 (like 2:1 as an example) so that sales activity doesn't entirely stop until the next plan period starts.

If the financial model supports it, the continuance of the accelerator rate is the most common approach. This translates into a very simple plan that delivers the message to keep selling and be rewarded at the known rate.

Weights and Measures

In your financial model, you may have determined more than one metric that was meaningful for the business to pursue. That may be net new accounts (new logos) and revenue, or it may be new business segments and new geographies/

territories, or bookings and profit margin. Whatever you have selected needs to be weighed against the alternatives based on the magnitude of importance. In other words, which metric is the one that the organization would absolutely have to achieve while missing all the others? Which one is the top, and by what difference in rank? This is where we get into weightings.

Let's suppose that new account logos and revenue is your priority. Revenue is very important, but you also need more new customers to secure additional funding. At this moment, logos matter more by a weighting because of this immediate need on the part of the organization. Understand that this will change and evolve over time, and the weighting evolves along with it. While revenue matters, the magnitude of it, by comparison, is lessened. So you may choose to use a plan that is 70% on new logos and 30% on revenue. This way there is focus on new business, but not entirely at the expense of revenue. There are a multitude of different measures that go into an incentive plan, and they are unique and specific to your organization at a moment in time. The following year, the weighting may be 50/50 or 100% on revenue depending on the success of the plan and the pursuit of new business.

Best practice is to have three or fewer measures. Too many measures and there will be no focus or clarity of the job. Additionally, all measures should at least be 20% of the total target incentive. Any lesser amount and it will be perceived as either inaccessible or out of their control, which will also induce a lack of focus. It will essentially translate into wasted expense on your part and serve as an unnecessary distraction on the salesperson's part.

I recommend starting with a single measure for your first plan. As always, keep it simple. Whenever we first start out at creating a new habit or trying to achieve something difficult, we want to start with small, simple steps that can be repeated. The new salesperson is charting new waters for your organization, and **a simpler path that clarifies the daily actions is of far greater value than a delightfully constructed and elegant sales incentive plan that is unnecessarily complex but achieves all sixteen of your desired objectives for your business on paper. That dog just won't hunt.**

If you're concerned about the other measures, this is a good time to introduce some process and business controls that surround them. As an example, if you select new logos only, establish a guideline for what deals are worth pursuing and what kind of business deals won't pay for themselves. This may be in the form of industry segmentation, establishing a discount authority, pricing guidelines, and profit thresholds to help manage the risks. Not everything has to be built into the sales incentive plan. In fact, I would advocate for it not to.

<u>Terminology Recap</u>

Accelerator

An increase in the rate of pay that occurs at a certain level of performance. Generally, this starts after the achievement of 100% of the target performance objective.

Deal Cap

The maximum amount of pay on any single transaction

Leverage

The sales incentive that would be paid out for performance between target and the point of excellence. It is represented as a multiple of the target incentive

Pay Curve

The slope of the line of the rate of pay throughout all levels of performance. Think of performance being the x-axis and payout being the y-axis. The pay curve represents the relationship between the two. In a fixed rate plan, this is a straight line, representing a fixed rate of pay for every unit of measured performance (activity completed, dollar of revenue acquired, or percentage point of margin sold, etc)

Plan Cap

Maximum amount of pay under the construct of the plan

Point of Excellence

The point on the pay curve that represents the 90th percentile of salespersons' performance levels

Rate of Pay

The amount of pay per unit of measurement. This encompasses the relationship between performance and payout at any point along the pay curve.

Target

A point on the pay curve that represents 100% payout and 100% performance or (100%, 100%)

Target Incentive

The sales incentive amount paid for achieving 100% of sales performance objectives

Threshold

The point at which pay for performance starts. The threshold point should sit somewhere between 0% and 100% performance levels. It can be zero which essentially means no threshold.

Zero

The first point on the pay curve; represented by (0%,0%) for zero level of payout and zero level of performance

<u>Homework</u>

1. Which type of sales plan makes the most sense for your organization? Why?
2. Review your objectives again and decide how you want to weigh them against each other.
3. Decide if you will be able to afford an accelerator. If so, what level is economical?

Chapter 7:
Period of Measurement
and Timing of Payout

*There is timing in everything. Timing in strategy
cannot be mastered without a great deal of
practice.*
- Miyamoto Musashi

*The two most important warriors are patience and
time.*
- Leo Tolstoy

TIMING IS EVERYTHING! DETERMINING THE LENGTH of time for the period of measurement of performance and the timing of payout of the sales incentives are two important aspects of compensation design.

Period of measurement

The period of measurement is the frequency of the performance periods within a sales incentive plan. For instance: annual, semi-annual, quarterly, or monthly. All of these periods of measurement may sit inside of a single incentive plan or may be independent periods entirely. As an example, performance objectives may be set monthly, and the period of measurement resets each month, but those 12 different periods of measurement are communicated inside of an overarching annual sales incentive plan.

Most organizations have an annual plan because that is how their financial budgets are established. You don't necessarily have to follow the annual plan model, but you want to take the time to document why you select what you do. This chapter will cover some of the considerations that you should account for in that decision-making process. It is helpful to explore how timing of performance periods within the plan can be of benefit to both the organization and the salesperson. You will want to think about some of the elements I will outline and the potential disincentives that are created by not being mindful of the impact associated with your decision. There are many factors that influence the selection of a performance period.

I'll cover it in greater detail below, but first, let's briefly cover payment timing.

<u>Timing of Payout</u>

The timing of payout is about selecting the frequency of administration of sales incentive and the release of cash to the salesperson. It is about both the determination of and calculation of payments associated with performance under the sales plan and how you want to schedule the payments over time associated with that performance. As an example, you will need to decide if you payout monthly, quarterly, or annually. This may be true for all components, or some of the components, of the sales incentive plan. You will need to decide on the pay cycles as well as what performance outcomes or levels of performance trigger a payout. Additionally, you will have to understand how you want to release the funds associated with the amount that is calculated for payout. Will you pay 100% of everything up front, delay a portion based on cash received, or clarify a set a schedule of disbursement? This ultimately equates to clarifying for the salesperson when incentives are earned as well as paid.

The organization has to decide on the timing of administration. Administration refers to the process of collecting performance data and determining the amounts eligible to be processed for payment under the sales incentive plan. There should be a connection between the cash coming in, the cash going out, and sales compensation administration timing. This is an extension of your financial model and certainly an important aspect for sustainability. You want to explore the relationship between the expected revenue and the commission expense. This is important from an accrual accounting perspective, but probably more so a cash flow perspective as you are getting started. The timing of expected cash inflows associated with deals procured should be understood when contemplating the cash outflows associated with the commission expenses from that same transaction. Administration is an important aspect for the future because of the on-going administrative burden to manage, calculate, and disburse payments, but also how it is used to motivate, retain, and attract talent. Additionally, it will be very challenging for your sales team to manage changes in cash flow. **You can always get more aggressive with payment timing but it is not as easy to ratchet it back down if you start out aggressive**. What I mean is that 100% payment of sales incentive at the time of closing business is quite aggressive. It will attract talent and likely retain talent because it is very competitive. However, it is quite difficult to maintain as the business gets more complex, and changing the rules later on will be more painful for those that lived through the "good ole' days." In my experience, I've seen it do more harm than good if you are building your business with the long-term in mind.

If you landed on the simple plan we covered in the earlier chapters, the one with the threshold at zero, then payout would commence once performance against the objective took place. If you select some other mechanics of triggering payout, then you will need to translate performance achievement to pay for your salesperson. That means explicitly documenting a schedule of administration and disbursements in your sales plan. It will also help to explain the "why" behind your decisions, and if they are at first perceived to be unfavorable, share how the payment timing can improve over time with more data and/or improved deal quality. Engage the salesperson as a business partner in the growth and pursuit of business, rather than treating them as merely an employee, and you will have better results.

In the process of determining the period of measurement and timing of payout, there are multiple factors to consider. These decisions will be unique and specific to your sales process and your business. The considerations include:

- Average sales cycle length
- Distribution of transactions
- Ability to influence timing of buyer's decision
- Cash dependency of the organization
- Impact from total pay and mix

The intersection of these different factors should be used to determine timing under the sales incentive plan.

Period of Measurement Continued
Average sales cycle length

The best practice for the period of measurement is that it should correspond with the ability of the salesperson to manage the transaction within it (or at least the components they manage in the sales cycle). It should include multiple opportunities for the salesperson to participate in deals during that period. For example, do not select a period of measurement that is a month when the normal sales cycle is six to eight months in length. That measurement time frame does not allow the salesperson a chance to participate with any consistency in each of the individual monthly periods of measurement. Essentially that decision would lock them out of the sales incentive and only serve to frustrate rather than motivate.

Essentially, for the period of time you select, the salesperson should have the ability to do their job from end to end. They should also be able to make multiple attempts to close/move business forward and have the capacity to influence the timing of future deals (pull in) to close within the present period. This is about influence, velocity, and variability of performance.

In an ideal world, a shorter sales cycle would translate into more transactions where more revenue is coming into the organization more quickly. That shorter business cycle should correspond to a shorter performance period and quicker disbursement of sales incentive payout.

Generally, salespeople participate in a one-year or less sales incentive plan. That's what makes a sales incentive plan a short-term incentive. For those businesses with sales cycles outside of the one-year length, or that are in multi-year sales cycles, the short-term incentive design is dramatically different and should focus on the incremental movement of the deal. Simply break down the sales cycle of the long-term or enterprise-level deals into milestones. Consider these distinct incremental sales cycles and focus on what can be controlled by the salesperson at each step in each micro-sales cycle or process. For instance, you may consider an alignment to the completion of sales stages, approvals, or acknowledgements of sales progression by the customer depending on the formality of your sales process.

As a general rule, the longer the sales cycle length, the longer the period of measurement.

Distribution of Transactions

The reason distribution of transactions matters is because the salesperson should have the opportunity to sell in each period of measurement. If your business is focused exclusively on procuring business in a single annual event of very heavily weighted seasonality, then you either need to acknowledge that with shorter focused periods of measurements that are weighted to those periods of performance, or don't attempt to carve up the annual plan into smaller pieces. When there are extended periods during the year where the salesperson is not actively selling, short-term incentive has less value.

Suppose that there are two annual conventions which are where 95% of your business comes from. Now all the work throughout the year is preparing demonstrations, producing and sharing marketing collateral, setting up meetings for the event, and ensuring samples of the product are available. If 95% of the business comes in during conventions that may only happen 4 days twice a year, then an annual sales plan won't do much to motivate or retain talent. You will need to look at alternatives like productivity bonuses leading up to the events or one-time payments for the significant biannual performance based on the magnitude of procured business. Either way, the disconnect from regularity of performance doesn't fit well into the traditional sales incentive plan.

Now if there are, instead, six conferences distributed throughout the year, the salesperson will have the opportunity to sell more regularly, achieve objectives, and exceed target incentive levels.

Ability to influence

If a salesperson doesn't have the ability to influence the timing of a deal closure, there's little reason for splitting up an annual plan into smaller performance periods. If a salesperson cannot sway a customer to buy earlier or change their expectations on the timing of the close of a deal, there is little reason to construct shorter measurement periods and/or make available the upside opportunities that would go along with those shortened measurement periods.

Let's suppose your business only bids to a single market segment. There is a very formal process where RFPs are managed through a prescriptive bid review, and the contracts are all done simultaneously to align with the budgetary or fiscal cycle of these businesses. Because your salesperson is locked out of influencing that timing process, there is no benefit to constructing a performance period that assumes timing of the deal can be influenced. You can choose to offer incentives to accelerate deals, but if the salesperson doesn't feel capable of--and you can validate that they are incapable of--accelerating the closure of business transactions, then you are only creating a morale issue where your salesperson feels disempowered and frustrated by the constant reminder of money that is out of reach. It is not a recipe for success.

Payout continued
Cash dependency

Cash dependency is all about the financial viability of the organization from the transactions that the salesperson is acquiring. As with any organization, some deals are better than others. Some are more profitable, and some have better payment terms than others. In an ideal world, this would be a non-issue, but the awareness of the cash flow from the types of transaction that the organization will experience, and how the organization will fund the payment of sales incentive, is a very practical point to be validated. This, of course, goes back to the financial modeling done in Chapter 1, but it is worth an additional emphasis because we want to shine more light on the business realities.

At what point in time will you have all the cash necessary to pay the sales incentive on a "normal" or "average" deal? How quickly after the close of the deal or the signature of the contract does cash start to come in, and when is all cash in? What level of variability exists between a great deal and a bad deal, but still a deal you plan to accept? How does that change the prior answers on cash receipt?

If there is a relatively limited variability in your distribution of deals, then a standard process of cash disbursement is ideal. And since your position is clear and known, you can afford to be more aggressive. If not, then a payout schedule based on percentage of cash received or deal quality levels may work out nicely.

Overall, **the best practice for payout is that you connect the financial reward to performance as quickly as you can afford to do so.** It is simple, positive reinforcement. You will have to temper that with the practicalities of a growing business.

Impact from total pay and mix

Lastly, let's talk about the impact of cash on motivation, and how that can be used. Generally, for roles with relatively low total target cash or high percentage of pay at risk, the sales incentive is a far more significant motivator. If you want to ensure that those incentive funds are used effectively, then you will need to connect them to the quick release of cash when performance justifies it. For those salespersons that are heavily reliant, at a personal level, with the cash flow from performance, payout should be more frequent.

Additionally, the more significant the risk the salesperson is taking on as a percentage of their total target cash compensation, the more frequent the opportunity they should have to gain the rewards for overperformance. It is my belief that this should apply to both performance periods and cash disbursement. Philosophically, the more risk they are taking on for the organization, the more they should have access to upside potential because of that risk. The underlying philosophy is simply ensuring the alignment of reward to risk levels.

I crafted a few scenarios to help illustrate how the considerations of timing impact the decisions on period of measurement and timing of payout.

Aspects of Timing

Three Scenarios

Scenario 1

Scenario Description:
Direct to consumer, in-person sales of internet and television packages at warehouse store

Average sales cycle length:
<1 day

Distribution of transactions:
Regular, weekly opportunities

Ability of salesperson to influence timing of buyer's decision:
Yes

Cash dependency of the organization:
Limited risk, if services are scheduled and credit card is taken upfront;
About 20% cancellation rate on service appointments

Impact from pay mix:
30% base/70% variable, relatively low TTC

Recommendation on Timing

Period of Measurement:
Monthly

Timing of Payout:
Monthly frequency; 100% payout upfront

Notes on recommendations:
Cancellations usually happen within 72 hours of initial appointment; Measure performance in arrears by two weeks to limit the impact of cancellations on payout

Scenario 2

Scenario Description:
Inside sales of hardware components to existing customers

Average sales cycle length:
3-5 weeks

Distribution of transactions:
Regular, but heavier towards end of quarter

Ability of salesperson to influence timing of buyer's decision:
Yes

Cash dependency of the organization:
Some risk, with delay of cash from invoice in the 60 to 90-day timeframe; Limited to risk on receiving payment, simply delayed cash inflow

Impact from pay mix:
55% base/45% variable, competitive TTC for role

Recommendation on Timing

Period of Measurement:
Quarterly

Timing of Payout
Monthly frequency; 100% payout upfront if deposit collected, otherwise tiered payout with some delay (example of 50% upfront, 50% in 90 days)

Notes on recommendations
Tie payout schedule to deal quality levels; this level of clarity will improve cash position or acceleration of revenue recognition over time

Scenario 3

Scenario Description:
Field-based, business to business, technical software sales

Average sales cycle length:
7-10 months

Distribution of transactions:
Semi-Regular, heavier at end of each fiscal half

Ability of salesperson to influence timing of buyer's decision:
No

Cash dependency of the organization:
High risk, significant sized deals with long-term contracted milestone payments associated with implementation

Impact from pay mix:
70% base/30% variable, high TTC given specialization

Recommendation on Timing

Period of Measurement:
Annual

Timing of Payout
Quarterly frequency; 34% upfront, 33% in 3 months, 33% in 6 months

Notes on recommendations:
The key is to establish predictable payout schedule regardless of the complexity of the business

To be clear, these are examples of periods of measure-ment and timing of payout that may work in these specific scenarios. If your organization happens to resemble one of these, and you end up with a different decision, it doesn't mean you are wrong. You have to decide what is best for your organization based on the information you have available. You have to walk the fine line between competitiveness and affordability for the long-run. I would just advocate for simplicity in your decisions wherever possible.

Homework
1. What is your period of measurement? How did you decide it?
2. What is your timing of payout?
3. How does cashflow influence your decisions? Will that change over time?

Chapter 8:
Putting it all together

If you don't know where you are going, you'll end up someplace else.

-   Yogi Berra

Everyone has a plan until they get punched in the mouth

-   Mike Tyson

WHILE WRITING THIS BOOK, I RECOGNIZED that there was a need to illustrate a few examples as a reference guide to cover what really is a complex topic. I selected three sales jobs that should help illustrate how all the pieces from the preceding chapters are put together to design the compensation plan for that particular job. These are hypothetical situations, and more likely than not, your particular situation won't be a perfect match. Don't expect it to. Any sales incentive design and the underlying job content of the position will be specific to your job requirements, your market, and your business environment.

The three jobs I selected are a Business Development Representative (BDR), an Account Manager (AM) and an Inside Sales Executive (ISE). I have provided a bit of a backstory on each to help illustrate why I made the recommendations I did.

JobTitle:
Business Development Representative (BDR)

Job Content-
Role Description:

This role is focused on the development of new leads and qualifying leads coming from marketing. The expectation of the job is to move a lead to qualified status and establish rapport with the customer with the use of collateral, webinars, and other means. The measure of success and hand off in the sales cycle is having the lead converted to a sales qualified opportunity. The activity metric is meetings with the prospective customer.

Further Job Content:

Telephone-based; Product-specific and geography focused territory; New business only; Associate degree or comparable experience required; Proven ability to influence required; Strong written and verbal communication required; Knowledge of solution selling or sales process desired.

Market Competitiveness –

Base Salary: $64,000
Target Incentive: $16,000
Total Target Cash: $80,000 (80/20 mix)

Internal Equity –
Job Valuation:

You will want to compare the compensation data with your other staff and the relative value that this role serves in the organization in comparison to other jobs

Sales Incentive Plan Example based on collected job data

Design Component: Objectives

Design Elements:

Financial Objective or Activity Objective

Recommendation:

Meetings & Sales Qualified Opportunities (SQO)

Further Explained:

Meetings are an activity that is fully within their control and has significant volume to measure over time. I also selected the SQOs as a measurement of quality (validated in the process of hand off). The intention is to capture both quantity and quality of work where possible.

Design Component: Plan Mechanics

Design Elements:

Plan Type

Recommendation:
Rate of pay per unit of activity
Further Explained:
A fixed amount per unit will clarify the daily objective of the role.

Design Elements:
Measure 1
Recommendation:
SQOs (8/quarter)
Further Explained:
Quarterly Target of SQOs (lower volume but higher value to the organization). Built in expected conversion rate.

Design Elements:
Weighting 1
Recommendation:
60%
Further Explained:
$9,600 per year / $2,400 per quarter / $300 per SQO

Design Elements:
Measure 2
Recommendation:
Meetings (32/quarter)
Further Explained:
Quarterly Target of Meetings (higher volume but lower value to the organization)

Design Elements:
Weighting 2
Recommendation:
40%
Further Explained:
$6,400 per year / $1,600 per quarter / $50 per meeting

Design Component: Pay Curve

Design Elements:
Threshold
Recommendation:
No threshold; Payout from first activity registered
Further Explained:
This is a simple plan that emphasizes payout for performance. Without a clear distribution of known performance, it is an unfair proposition to set a threshold. This is a simple plan that emphasizes payout for performance. Without a clear distribution of known performance, it is an unfair proposition to set a threshold.

Design Elements:
Accelerator
Recommendation:
1.5x

Further Explained:

Both measures to increase the rate of pay from 100% to 150% of quarterly targets to incentivize over performance of activity. Because the salesperson is carrying limited risk in the role, there is limited upside potential.

Design Elements:

Point of Excellence

Recommendation:

150%

Further Explained:

Without additional information, 150% is a good default, especially where an activity-based plan is in use

Design Elements:

Rate above Point of Excellence

Recommendation:

SQOs Uncapped / Meetings Capped at 150%

Further Explained:

There is declining marginal value in the quantity of meetings within a quarter. Because there is limited gauge on the quality of those meetings being booked, it is best to limit the upside. SQOs, on the other hand, are of greater value as they have a higher probability to convert to revenue and should be emphasized with greater value, given that they have been validated in the sales process

Design Component: Period of Measurement

Design Elements:
Sales Cycle Length, Distribution of
Transactions, Ability to Influence
Recommendation:
Quarterly
Further Explained:
Average sales cycle length will be 2-5 weeks.
Meetings will occur regularly throughout the
week. SQOs will be less frequent but should
occur monthly. The BDR will use persuasion in
the act of establishing meetings and provide
thorough discovery and validation in order to
achieve qualification of sales opportunities.

Design Component: Timing of Payout

Design Elements:
Cash dependency, Impact from Pay mix
Recommendation:
Monthly / No deferred incentive
Further Explained:
This is an activity-based sales plan with a target
incentive of $4,000 per quarter tied to
quarterly objectives. The plan will be
independent quarterly measurement periods of
performance meaning opportunity for quarterly
acceleration based on performance. This role is
an investment and not accountable for
procurement of revenue. There is no benefit to

delay the payment of sales incentive.

Further Comments

For BDR roles, expect improvements on productivity and conversion rates over time based on time in job and success in role. Regularly review the definitions of the objectives as well as the specific target volumes for modification and rebalancing.

Title:
Account Manager (AM)

Job Content-
Role Description:

This role is focused on the development of recurring business with an existing account base. The expectation of the job is to maintain relationships with influential staff, administrators, and decision-makers to secure revenue for the office supply business. The measure of success is exceeding the monthly revenue quota and annual revenue objectives. An activity that is believed to support this success is securing long-term contract agreements. The role is also tasked with developing opportunities at those existing accounts with new/incremental portfolio items like copy machines and off-site print work.

Further Job Content:

Field-based; Account assigned territory; Existing business only; Focused on procurement of exclusive office supply contracts and maximizing revenue at each account. 2+ years of experience in Customer Support, Services, or Sales required; Proven track record of performance against financial objectives; Ability to persuade decision makers required; Good verbal communication, business etiquette, and physical presentation skills required; Ability to lift boxes up to 40 pounds in the normal course of business required; Driver's license required; Ability to travel approximately up to 80% of time; No overnight travel required; Familiarity with inner workings of business office desired; Familiarity with office products is a plus.

Market Competitiveness –
Base Salary: $$56,000
Target Incentive: $24,000
Total Target Cash: $80,000 (70/30; fixed TI for role with base tied to experience)

Internal Equity –
Job Valuation:
You will want to compare the compensation data with your other staff and the relative value that this role serves in the organization in comparison to other jobs

Sales Incentive Plan Example based on collected job data

Design Component: Objectives

Design Elements:
Financial Objective or Activity Objective
Recommendation:
Revenue Target + Long-term contract agreements
Further Explained:
The objective is to focus on the relationships at business offices and secure contracts. Actual

performance of the value of those contracts is in the revenue they provide to the organization. As the organization evolves, there is opportunity to shift focus towards growth of baseline revenue. Additionally, there is benefit to securing long-term agreements to normalize revenue projections for the organization.

Design Component: <u>Plan Mechanics</u>

Design Elements:
Plan Type
Recommendation:
Commission + Activity Bonus
Further Explained:
Fixed Rate of commission for revenue / Bonus per agreement

Design Elements:
Measure 1
Recommendation:
Monthly Revenue ($100K per month)
Further Explained:
Actual revenue recognized in month from assigned accounts.

Design Elements:
Weighting 1
Recommendation:
80%

Further Explained:

$1,600 per month variable / 1.6% commission rate

Design Elements:

Measure 2

Recommendation:

Long-term contracts (8 per year)

Further Explained:

Long-term contract agreements over 12 months in length. Half credit for agreements 6-12 months. No credit for agreements under six months.

Design Elements:

Weighting 2

Recommendation:

20%

Further Explained:

$4,800 per year variable / $600 per contract

Design Component: Pay Curve

Design Elements:

Threshold

Recommendation:

50%

Further Explained:

0% payout under 50% monthly performance. 50% payout at 50% performance. Since there is an existing run rate of revenue there are well established revenue objectives tied to each of the existing accounts, a threshold is appropriate.

Design Elements:
Accelerator
Recommendation:
1.20x
Further Explained:
20% uplift on all monthly revenue over target. Reset each month.

Design Elements:
Point of Excellence
Recommendation:
130%
Further Explained:
The expectation is that the top performers (90th percentile) would only be able to achieve performance levels over 130% of monthly target

Design Elements:
Rate above Point of Excellence
Recommendation:
1.20x
Further Explained:
Flat rate acceleration continued beyond point of excellence.

Design Component: Pay Curve

Design Elements:
Sales Cycle Length, Distribution of
Transactions, Ability to Influence
Recommendation:
Monthly for Revenue / Quarterly for long-term
contracts
Further Explained:
Average sales cycle length will be less than one
month. Revenue is expected to continue and
grow with the influence of this role. The AM
will have full capacity to persuade in expanding
the portfolio of offerings and pursue signatures
of long-term contracts to solidify the formality
of partnership relationships. Transactions
should come in throughout the month.

Design Component: Timing of Payout

Design Elements:
Cash dependency, Impact from Pay mix
Recommendation:
Monthly for Revenue / Quarterly for long-term
contracts
Further Explained:
The plan will be independent monthly
measurement periods of performance meaning
opportunity for monthly acceleration based on
performance. There is little to no benefit to
delay the payment of sales incentive for actual

revenue delivered. Long-term contracts are a valuable leading indicator but also don't carry the same weight of value to the organization unless they deliver on revenue. There is benefit to ensuring they are of value to the organization with quarterly bonus payouts. Quarterly bonus payouts for the long-term contracts illustrate they carry a lesser value than actual revenue. Since they are a long-term investment, it is reasonable to pay less frequently.

Further Comments

Existing-client account managers are expected to grow revenue beyond baseline and are paid well for executing long term agreements. Because there is an aggressive compensation cost for a line of business that has tighter margins, I am not proposing an aggressive accelerator. The 6.7% compensation cost of revenue is calculated by taking the total target cash compensation of 80,000 and dividing it by the performance objective of 1,200,000 Revenue.

Title:
Inside Sales Executive (ISE)

Job Content-
Role Description:
The role is to manage the end-to-end sales cycle selling cloud-based software in the small and medium businesses (SMBs) segment. The expectation of the job is to pursue new business opportunities in the new geographic area that the business is investing in for expansion of services. The measure of success is in annual recurring revenue (ARR) and the quantity of new accounts secured. The sale is semi-complex and there are a number of existing competitors in the space. Expected to develop own leads and manage full sales cycle.

Further Job Content:
Telephone-based; Product-specific and geography focused territory; New business only; Bachelor's degree required; 2+ years of sales experience required; Ability to gain consensus from multiple and diverse stakeholders in smaller and medium-sized organizations required; Experience managing entire sales cycle desired; Knowledge of reward and recognition software and market desired.

Market Competitiveness –
Base Salary: $72,000
Target Incentive: $48,000

Total Target Cash: $120,000 (60/40; fixed TI for role with base tied to experience)

Internal Equity –
Job Valuation:
You will want to compare the compensation data with your other staff and the relative value that this role serves in the organization in comparison to other jobs

Sales Incentive Plan Example based on collected job data

Design Component: Objectives

Design Elements:
Financial Objective or Activity Objective
Recommendation:
Annual Recurring Revenue (ARR)
Further Explained:
The objective is to pursue new business subscriptions. Because this is a new geographic segment and the transaction sizes will be relatively the same there is not a need to also have a new logo objective. Additionally, at this point the business is just focused on the initial contract with new customers rather than worrying about term length over their standard 12-month contracts, so we will not be emphasizing longer term deals.

Design Component: Plan Mechanics

Design Elements:
   Plan Type
Recommendation:
   Commission Rate
Further Explained:
   Commission rate tied to ARR performance

Design Component: Pay Curve

Design Elements:
   Measure 1
Recommendation:
   ARR ($300,000 per quarter)
Further Explained:
   Defined as the 12-month contract value of the subscription

Design Elements:
   Weighting 1
Recommendation:
   100%
Further Explained:
   $12,000 per quarter at target / $48,000 per year

Design Elements:
   Threshold
Recommendation:
   None

Further Explained:

Instead of a threshold, there will be a rate of 2.4% from 0-50% and 5.6% from 50-100% of quota

Design Elements:

Accelerator

Recommendation:

2x

Further Explained:

Rate will increase to 8% >100% (base rate is $12,000 / $300,000 or 4%)

Design Elements:

Point of Excellence

Recommendation:

150%

Further Explained:

Expect it to be 150% or higher, based on existing business practices in the other geographies

Design Elements:

Rate above Point of Excellence

Recommendation:

2.5x

Further Explained:

Rate will increase to 10% over 150% (base rate is $12,000 / $300,000 or 4%)

Design Component: <u>Timing of Payout</u>

Design Elements:
Sales Cycle Length, Distribution of
Transactions, Ability to Influence
Recommendation:
Quarterly
Further Explained:
There is currently a 2-to-3-month sales cycle
length; Expect transactions to occur monthly
after initial development of pipeline occurs;
There is a clear ability to persuade buyers and
demonstrated experience in influencing the
timing of transactions

Design Component: <u>Timing of Payout</u>

Design Elements:
Cash dependency, Impact from Pay mix
Recommendation:
Quarterly
Further Explained:
This is an independent quarterly plan. The
accelerators will reset quarterly. Payment
timing is best aligned to quarterly to reconcile
full performance level with payment. Because
this is projected annual revenue value, it is
appropriate to delay some of the payment
timing to ensure revenue/expense alignment
but these are guaranteed contracts so the
quarterly pay cycle should have sufficient lag

time built in to collect cash. If cash becomes a greater issue, then propose a short-term incentive for upfront payment from clients rather than monthly or develop that as a standard contracting expectation and process

Further Comments

The ISE role will evolve based on success in the specific task of geographic penetration. The accelerators are intentionally aggressive to prompt quick and regular business development each quarter. There is very little variable cost of software, so more aggressive accelerators are common practice. Additionally, after the initial runway, cash should not be an issue as many customers will be billed and pay full annual fee upfront. The structure uses a lower commission rate rather than a threshold. This reduced rate addresses paying the ISE from dollar one of performance, but also protects the organization with a certain minimum level of performance necessary to fund this expansion effort.

As I shared at the beginning of the chapter, these probably won't fit your needs exactly. The unique combination of the needs of the sales function within your current environment and the selection of the important metrics under the constraints of your current financial model will create a sales role and incentive model that will be specific to you and your organization. That being said, I hope that they provided an illustration of the decisions needed and options available in creating a meaningful, overall sales compensation design offering to effectively attract, retain, and motivate the right salesperson for your organization.

Homework
1. Take the design components from the grid and populate a few options for your new sales role?
2. Decide if you need to adjust the initial decisions to reinforce competitiveness or reduce because of financial constraints.

Chapter 9: Sustainability

Sustained success means making the greatest possible impact over the longest period of time.
- Marcus Buckingham

One can choose to go back toward safety or forward toward growth. Growth must be chosen again and again; fear must be overcome again and again.
- Abraham Maslow

THE INTENT OF THIS BOOK IS TO PROVIDE a guide to building a compensation plan for your first salesperson. Hopefully, by now you have a better handle on the steps and details involved in setting up your organization, and your first salesperson, for success.

1. We first looked at culture and ensuring alignment of the role in pursuit of your organization's strategy.
2. We then validated affordability and built an understanding of the numbers that go into the financial decisions behind a successful sales position.
3. We then spent the time to really dig deep into the role and responsibility of the sales job. As you may recall, the takeaway was a job description that was uniquely catered to your organization in pursuit of what you truly need to be successful given the information gleaned from the prior chapters.
4. Next, we spent some time understanding the labor market dynamics and what internal equity means as your organization evolves. With those data sources, you should be well prepared to have a good sense of what the sales job will cost.
5. In chapter 5, we began looking at sales objectives and emphasized the connection to your financial model while at the same time being fair and achievable to ensure long-term viability of the

sales position.

6. After finalizing objectives, we dug into the varying aspects of the pay curve and what we wanted to pay at all of the different levels of performance.

7. Before putting it all together, we finished up with timing. The period of measurement and payout timing were covered to assist in aligning the performance and cash flow of the individual salesperson to the financial performance and cash flow of the organization.

Throughout this book we reiterated the need to revisit the financial model and budget to ensure affordability of the position. You should be asking yourself: Do I need a salesperson to meet my financial objectives? What can I afford to pay a salesperson?

Additionally, we discussed the need to remain relevant and competitive in the labor market. You do this by clarifying the job explicitly and collecting data points to help validate compensation levels **regularly**. Be sure to review the pay mix and total target cash compensation on a normal cadence. Once you are beyond survivability, you will be able to shift focus to sustainability.

A further note on pay. The current labor market (as of early 2022) is presently quite aggressive, and I do expect it to stay that way for the next few years. Any decision about pay will need to temper affordability with what is competitive. Over the last many years, the base salary expectations of sales employees have increased substantively. Sales roles demand much higher base salaries than in the past. With more guaranteed pay, there would be a logical inclination for lesser pay at risk. While that may not be the case in your individual market, for many it means less emphasis on management by incentive.

Many think of sales people as being "coin operated," and in the past, organizations were able to get by without fixing the challenges of the work or improving management. You do not have that luxury. With greater emphasis on base salary because of the shift in labor market dynamics, you will have to understand that the path to sustainability is also about ensuring a positive work atmosphere, creating purposeful work, an environment of recognition, clarity of responsibilities, and the ability to see a path to success and performance. **True sustainability involves continual improvements in culture, process, and leadership**.

Lastly, the steps we have taken thus far are meant for the original financial model, sales strategy, and job content for this first hire. Once the team expands, jobs evolve, or the company changes its strategy, the exercise will need to be repeated to ensure alignment of compensation with objectives. This is absolutely necessary in order for your organization to incentivize the right behaviors and actions in pursuit of optimal outcomes.

I wish you well in your endeavors of growth and sustainability!

Afterword

Have no fear of perfection, you'll never reach it
- Salvador Dali

AS STEVEN LANDSBURG APTLY PUT IT when talking about economics, "People respond to incentives. The rest is commentary." Incentives matter, and we are ultimately talking about both implicit and explicit incentives throughout this book as it relates to how the organization wants the salesperson to act, and how they are rewarded for those actions, whether good or bad. Ensuring that the sales plan and the incentive structure it creates aligns to the intentions of the organization is the purpose of this book.

This book is to aid as a guide in your pursuit of optimal outcomes for your organization. The difficulty is that this is always fleeting. Just like our lives, we are constantly in an environment of change that must be revisited and reconsidered based on the changes of the world around us. Sales incentive plans are no different. Once something changes in the business, they will need to be revisited to ensure they still align with the desired outcomes, and that the incentive structure is still meaningful enough to attract, motivate, and retain the right talent necessary to accomplish the financial objectives that you have outlined for your organization.

I wish you all the success in the world for your endeavors towards growth. If you would like to talk through any topics discussed in this book, please do not hesitate to reach out to me at **christopher@salescompguy.com**

Acknowledgements

Acknowledging the good that you already have in your life is the foundation for all abundance.

- Eckhart Tolle

Nearly two years ago, in the early days of the Covid-19 pandemic, I had the pleasure of meeting George Wang. George is the Co-Founder and Director of an organization called SIRUM that focuses on reducing barriers to health for underserved populations through prescription drug donations. We were introduced through a mutual acquaintance because the organization needed some help bringing on their first sales role. George's mission is an outstanding one and is quite meaningful to the future of healthcare, so my challenge was to add value where I could and think of what he needed to know in this endeavor to grow the organization with a new sales staff. If it wasn't for George, I am not sure I would have taken the time to work through this topic and ultimately write this book. Thank you, George!

This book would not have been possible without the help and support from so many people. Abby, thank you for your edits and being the best accountability partner I could ask for. Tonya, thank you for all the design work on the book and the brand. A special thank you to all my advanced readers for all your feedback and guidance. Thank you, John Rubino, Rich Marra, John Hood, Ali Ghiassi, Lauren Spencer, Kelley Schudy, and George Wang,

An additional thank you all the others than influenced my evolution of thought on the subject of sales compensation and unknowingly influenced the concepts in this book. There are innumerable people that contributed to my development in so many ways. For all of you and those I have unintentionally left off, thank you from the bottom of my heart.

Lastly, thank you to all the founders, entrepreneurs, side-gig pursuers, coaches, speakers, consultants, and creatives that keep building businesses and hustling to get to a better version of themselves. This book is for you!

About the author

Success isn't a result of spontaneous combustion. You must set yourself on fire.

- Arnold Glasgow

CHRISTOPHER GOFF has over 15 years of Sales Operations and Compensation experience including a background in the Healthcare, Software & Technology, and Contract Research industries. He is currently pursuing his MBA from Rasmussen University and holds a Master's degree in Economics from North Carolina State University, and a B.S. in Finance from Catawba College. He is also a Certified Sales Compensation Professional (CSCP), Global Remuneration Professional (GRP), and Certified Compensation Professional (CCP).

The Rest of the Story

Thank you for taking the time to read the book in its entirety. It is my hope that you were able to find some valuable resources in this journey. As you've discovered, there is a lot of nuance to building and optimizing your sales compensation plans. But the good news is, you're not on your own.

For more information on the ins-and-outs of sales compensation, please check out my website at **https://www.salescompguy.com** and sign up for my bi-weekly newsletter .

Go to the Sales Comp Guy Website
https://www.salescompguy.com/.

If you want to talk one-on-one, reach out to me directly at **christopher@salescompguy.com**

www.ingramcontent.com/pod-product-compliance
Lightning Source LLC
Chambersburg PA
CBHW072315210326
41519CB00057B/5157